Life in the City

by Margie Burton, Cathy French, and Tammy Jones

I live in the city with my mom and dad.
I like to live in the city. There is so much
to see and do in the city.

This is where I
live. My building
has many homes in it.
I do not have a yard.
I play on the sidewalk
with my friends.

There are many stairs in my building.
I live on the top floor.

This is my friend. She lives
on the same floor as I do.

This is my dog.
I like to go
for a walk
with my dog
on my street.
I have to keep him
on a leash.

My mom and dad go to work every day.
My mom rides the train to work.
My dad walks to work. I ride
to school on a schoolbus.

Here is my dad
going to work.

The train is called a subway.

This is my bus.

We do not have a car. There are too many cars in the city. We walk, ride the bus, or take the train.

This is my school in the city. There are
not many trees around the building or
on the playground.

There are a lot of stores in the city.
My mom likes to shop in the stores
beside our home.

I like to go to play in this park.

This is the zoo in the city. I like to look at the monkeys.

I like to look at the elephants, too.

I do not like to look at the snakes.

This is where I like to go to read.

This is my library.

Sometimes, I go out to eat with my mom
and dad. I like to eat at this restaurant
in the city.

After we eat, we go to the store
to get ice cream.

When we get home, it is dark. I like
to go up to the top of my building.
I can see a long way. I like
the city at night!